Renaissance

Also by Ruth Forman *We Are the Young Magicians*

Beacon Press *Boston*

Ruth Forman

Renaissance

Beacon Press
25 Beacon Street
Boston, Massachusetts 02108-2892

Beacon Press books
are published under the auspices of
the Unitarian Universalist Association of Congregations.

The title and first two lines from "Don't Try to Kiss Me into
Shape" are from Chrystos, "Don't Try," published in *Dream On*
(Vancouver, B.C.: Press Gang Publications, 1991).

*Grateful acknowledgment is made to the journal in which these
poems first appeared:*

"Venus's Quilt"
The Drumming Between Us, vol. 1, no. 1 (Fall 1994)

"Give Me a Kiss"
The Drumming Between Us, vol. 1, nos. 1 and 2 (Fall 1994 and
Spring 1995)

03 02 01 00 99   8 7 6 5 4 3 2

Text design by Elizabeth Elsas
Composition by Wilsted & Taylor Publishing Services

Library of Congress Cataloging-in-Publication Data
Forman, Ruth.
      Renaissance / Ruth Forman.
          p.   cm.
      ISBN 0-8070-6840-3 (cloth)
      ISBN 0-8070-6841-1 (paper)
      I. Title.
   PS3556.07334R46   1998
   811'.54—dc21   97-20611

For Mom

DC Public Library

Author: Hand, Monica A.
Title: Me and Nina : poems
Item ID: 31172080676687
Date charged: 3/28/2016,
16:07
Date due: 4/18/2016,23:59

Author: Forman, Ruth.
Title: Renaissance
Item ID: 31172041199571
Date charged: 3/28/2016,
16:07
Date due: 4/18/2016,23:59

Thank you for using the
DC Public Library

If You Write Poetry

Go to the ground

it should make the ancestors put down their pipes
and let you tell the story
it should make the grandmothers rock
themselves like they rocked you
it should make your momma wonder
who you are
and your daddy feel
he's someplace real
like the root of your hair
and where you come from

Contents

Homecoming

Venus's Quilt

Renaissance

Young Black Question

We Walk

a bridge
between our parents' dreams
and vultures
between death's fingers
and the palms of the universe

Abraham Got All the Stars n the Sand

Daddy 43 but look 40
35 when he laugh
ma family big n pretty

Bo
look like smooth onyx stone
Randy look like
Florida sand
Winnie
the breath of honeysuckle
Leesha
a redwood tree
Peaches
look like plums
n Momma
sweet coconut meat
next to Daddy color of baking chocolate

n Jojo
she buckwheat honey
in the mornin
when Daddy grease n part her hair
for the ready red ribbons
glow so next to her skin

he
put twists in Leesha's
n Peaches get three thick braids
We always sing
different songs at the table

n Gramma let us do it
as she pour her coffee

watch them lil teeth shinin
thinkin
Abraham got all the stars n the sand
but she got all the rainbow.

Five

i can make mommy laugh
move the salt shaker when nobody lookin
i can change a red light to green
n make a ole lady wonder how um so smart
readin the aisles in the Stop n Shop

i can make grown men fall in love with me
n call fireflies out to play when the sun go down

i can braid ma own hair as well as Barbie's
even though hers don't hold
i can run fast as Daddy's car
when he leave to go back home

i can fall out a tree n land on ma feet
build a fort n
cook pepper n water soup for dinner

i'm five n just about all the magic i need

Ashley

Got two sandy braids
smile big as my eyes
n two knobby knees
but graceful as you please

hey give me some
raisins
peanut butter
celery
I'll whip you up a recipe
ants on a log
Ms. Mina I know they taste good but
save some for me

I like to laugh
Daddy flip me upside down in the kitchen
Bryan play applesticks most anywhere
Mommy call me between her knees at night

Lord gotta do something with this hair

I braid baby doll's while she braid mine
n stretch my legs to the far corners of the bed

got feet that will take me to Ohio
magination to take me even further
good spoonful of common sense
and all the way determination

I'm gramma Forman all over again
but in my own special way
two new arms to hug the future
with love that taste like oranges

Jus Enough to Keep On

Got a bus pass so i can ride
Shower to Shower so people don mind sittin next to me
a bed to sleep in
some lipstick n a brush
so i don't look like i jus rolled out

got a mind to bring me places i need to go
sense to keep me from places i don't
God to hold my hand
n a prayer to say thank you

sunglasses so i don't squint when the sky too bright
respect to take em off when you got somethin to say
skin dark to welcome the sun
hair curly to celebrate sweat

got a momma to love and a daddy i'm learnin to
world tangled enough to keep me busy
confidence to roll up my sleeves
n faith enough to keep on

jus enough to keep on

Haiku

Ma granbaby eight
bullet hole in his lef knee
for not runnin crack

Igotasonginmahead

n you can't catch it i'm too fast
step shoes you can't catch me
young brothas comin up n comin down comin up n fallin out
comin up sellin out comin up gettin out

igotasonginmahead you can't catch it 1995
n five years comin like a rainstorm
mommy can't catch herself in our times
we too young n electronic
here come the guns on the tracks on the arms America
rumblin ma head like tombstones fallin
like Christ callin the righteous
like they comin all 2000 years of em

igotasonginmahead call in the millennium

sisters can't see where they walk
don't know what they feet look like so tight in platforms
igotasong i got a crack in ma evenin
crack the program
we too commercial
ma head ina swing ma soul ina sling
mommy can't see herself in ma times

igotasonginmahead gonna sing it to the future
since i don't know how much longer
i got this street

A Little Voice

God why you make me a voice
when i don't love to talk
hide if i cd in a pee stank corner
long as i had heavy shoes

but you have me speak
in the season of my grandmothers
curse
in the spice of my uncles

why bid me say what i have to say
among so many vines n broken glass
needles n bullet shells

who wd listen to such a journey of a child

Aye Nay

Who has ever written you a poem?

you eleven
older days come fast
words hit from the stereo harsh n hard
you nod your head to the beat

Aye Nay
who has ever spoken to you softly
n it be in style?
who ever kiss your cheek
n it be hip?
your name means *my eyes*
who ever said they beautiful
in front of a whole room n they agreed?

you just turned eleven
i don't know what the years coming look like
soon you enter a storm
i see the rumblings on you
black child in Los Angeles
endangered species
i would call all my people to stand
n make a circle around you
until you grown
i would carry you
if you behaved
but all i can do
is give you these words
soft as the morning when no one else notice

this is to tell you i see you

hold on to this poem
in your backpack
in your pocket
when bass too much
hard make you tired
or when you feel particularly un-unique
pull it out n read it

you eleven
soon entering another world
this is to keep you coming
this is to keep for the travel

Who Got Ma Head While They Hand in Ma Pocket
or
Shopping for Everything outside Ma Self

Who got ma head and what they doin with it
while they hand in ma pockets

interactive video big screen stereo never mind the soundtrack
who got ma brainwaves between the airwaves of cellular callers
and celluline microcapsule potions

who got they hand in ma pockets not big enough
got to go in ma next pants ma next day ma next month
who got ma car really who got ma road who got ma hair
lookin good for whose event
who got ma dress
next week imma pick it up
Columbia House got to buy that CD who got ma stereo
5-changer car player in the trunk where ma music
in ma head I whistle made it up ma self

I'm tired of namin tired of namin
Sony Nike Coke Sprite Obey Your Thirst 501s
on a violently changing billboard Crenshaw and 59th
Bud thing Baby Kool Camel Lights who got ma head Sega Sega
Sprint RC who Colt 45 it's the tiger Pink Relaxer who got it got it
Gangsta's Paradise St. Ives
Don't Blend In Beverly Center
all these in ma head and how do you get them out?

all this in a morning ride
I need a detox
but just to come out to the same thing

give me a sliver of the universe on ma plate
to soothe ma tired inside
I'm fightin for ma mind
who got ma head who got ma head
fightin for something I forget more and more
what I'm fightin
what I'm fightin
for

Graduate School

The book not so big
for you to get lost in the pages
perhaps you don't find yourself in them
cause they so thin
and you so thick like buckwheat honey

trust your footsteps
trust your eyes and tongue

start easy
one or two sentences per class
feel comfortable with the sound of your voice
in a small room ten people one large table

speak your heart they will hear
hearts speak to each other
even when minds don't listen
walk with your neck showing

and when afraid

trust your footsteps
trust your eyes and tongue
they come from a long place long time

if you can't find
the root in your spine
stand still and wait with your hand on a wall
listen to its negotiations with gravity

until you find the lava flow solid from your veins
harden your back
rise your throat and over

then
speak what you know without translation
stand without negotiation
and fight

like your spirit already knows

Los Angeles

Where do i fit
in this place of jagged puzzles
sky-high metal wide
as the ocean
Moses parted
with his red hands
how do i make myself/mold myself
into the curve of the freeways
place my hands on the mirrored buildings of fathers
and leave my fingerprints

everybody would like to say
"I was here"
hopscotch the stars by the Chinese Theatre
n get a foot stuck a hand stuck in wet cement
what does it mean
us wanting to make memory of ourselves
so badly
rushing into suicides n places
ready to eat our spirits whole
could it mean we just want to get through this life
ring a doorbell n run
tag a wall n move on

who will claim a space n go down with it
who willing to be a freeway
to be stuck
in the cement of a building

no
i would rather claim a stream
lay my bones easily upon the bottom

then say
ruth was here
as i whisper myself
home

Young Black Question

who to say
this sidewalk actually solid
who to say this sidewalk where to walk

ask you cuz i have so many questions
afraid to form them
with the air
i have partnership with silence

and many investors

Kin

Mother

The bottom of your feet tell me
you a sturdy woman
the kind who plant moons
in her children's dreams

Daughter

I have danced this dance
a million times still wonder
who give me my feet

The Williams Side of the Family

We all women here
big boned and sassy
been so since we dropped from our mamas

we all sisters here
long talk and evenin
early and work hard

we all mothers here
babies and patience full
quick tongue and love

we all children here
looking for God at the end of our prayers

How long for y'all to see
who we be
your relative
long long at the end of the dirt road
pot fulla collard greens
n waitin on company

Old Man Samuel

How many lovers do it take to get down one road?
and how much loneliness to appreciate a straightaway?
I have 11 women in ma name and no fingers for ma lips

We all have water waiting to spill
mine with no bucket
come rain and wheat fields grow me something nice
grow me a train cross California
and young girls' smiles
grow me poke salad like my mama useta make
and staircases
strong to hold you gainst the wind

I tell you I miss Georgia
young ladies in yellow hats and how do's
swing skirts in a bashful way
lowered eyes with stars beneath I tell you
if I could just go home again
raise ma feet upon the rail and smoke out into the fields
unravel ma dreams after dinnertime

if I could just bring Jean back again
braids uncommon ropes
clingin to her head
lettin go only at my touch
I guess too much
some days

they grew tighter and tighter
n ma fingers more and more loose
to wander under the skirts of
legs without faces

nothin like Blue Georgia Whiskey
nothin like the sky so low you blow the stars
like dandelions
now me I blow ma wishes to
exhaust and black automobiles
so many passin by I forget my own feet sometimes

ma legs yawn the way they useta tell a story
wonder if they could now

These young men walkin like they got so much to tell
or so much to hide
nobody look at the old men
there is more in ma half a step
than they got in a whole block's worth a stroll.

Sometime

it don't matter who you are
loneliness just come up n grab you
like a best friend

Sing to Me Evenin

calm and rockin
crickets and ladybugs
back in the grass tall
talk with each other

sing to me evenin
all your comfort of cloaked sky
time i give up my wrinkles to the end of the day
to be washed and pressed
ready for mornin

sing to me evenin
forgive me my troubles
let me sit in who i really am
if not for a minute so i can breathe

Aunt Thelma

I am already a thing of the past
my children hum me like a folktale
and the babies listen with wide eyes

they don't know I am the moon
more and more every day

step inside the kitchen window
when everybody sleep
and shine like I used to
when floors was waxed
shoes was new
night nothin but a sleeve
to slip my arms through
and try on the fit.

Me n this chair
now so much a part of me
hardly feel the need to get up

but I am the moon
more and more every day

3 am this kitchen a dance hall
all my memories
in a rhythm I can take
slow enough
for me to close
my eyes.

National Treasures
for Peter J. Harris

Let us name our national treasures
current as today's newspaper
come let us name our national treasures
our uncles our teachers our lovers of the soul
much as we name our criminals

the ones so sui generis they urge our own uniqueness
to seep through our pores
us little buds at the tips of our parents' fingers
reaching for a future they've never known

this is the time to sing the name of just one person
who make us want to see another day
hear her words and know
through the burnings and lynchings and breaking bones of history
on some plane carrying us through our days
everything's gonna be alright
I need my neighbor who I don't know very well
to give me a national treasure he hold dear to his heart
and if he have more
I will take them
like promises

I am serious as tears
rocking her baby's broken head on the sidewalk
serious as bullet shells and a blood-dusky sky
serious as this year and as much cocaine snorted into hell
i'm serious mama
like chains

I need me these treasures pinned on my walls
with stickpins and tacks and bubble gum

need their pictures and scribbled names on any kind of paper
one from each person on my block
one put on channel 9 every night
what she do unsung and workin overtime
what he do
why should it be they only celebrated in heaven?
we need to know them here

I need me names in buckets
fill my hands with they lives and breathe it in
like mint like sage
like time in my hands

need me the memories of each one in this city
if you have a national treasure give it to me
I have a national treasure
Roy Thomas. Sonia Sanchez. Anna Stevenson. Peter J. Harris.
    Afiya.
those ones you know like the restless song of a river
they keep this world going
and the babies alive

I need them in my life need them all
send them names to the *LA Times*
conquer my shaking head and set it straight
make me look for them in the street
that one?

like a junky need heroin and a lover need touch
I need it like the full spirit of a child

who will write the name of their national treasure
on a slip of paper?
we need to know them

I only wish that I could say it better.

Hand Me Your Palm

i trace a language
fingers touch skin slowly
wander your streams

somethin special bout hands
God gave them for more than picking things up
carved them to remind us
we have a long way to go

travelers we are
who've forgotten our packs
stop to build on the first dust heap we find
fill it with rock and wood and glass
breath a spirit through once in a while

traveler
what if we were to pack ourselves only
and continue downstream
leave the wood and her sisters behind
what would we take?

Reunion

Bring someone some hope
like a basket of good nectarines
to share n bite n
love the sweet

bring someone some Black hope
the kind that roll from Uncle Junior's laugh
n Aunt Bert's hands when she cookin

bring someone a slice of hope
like they come over to your house on Sunday afternoon
give a parlor a den a living room
fulla pictures a sisters cousins babies
n new schoolchildren
in your smile

give a worn chair to sit down in
your conversation
a tall glass of lemonade
in your handshake

give someone some hope today
like you need so badly
walkin the halls of your own home
like a strange place

reach into the living room inside you
and all you learn from the last generation
the one you step on they backs to be where you are

pull out the card games and barbeques
block parties and patios

let them come out the light in your eyes
for someone who need

you give to yourself in givin
that living room you walk
look more like the one on the inside
all them good folk
keepin you company

Even If You Grab a Piece of Time

conjure something glowing

take this day

you were born with
hands for spinning
talent for dreams and making them real

roll the hours like yarn
spin something that make you feel full
and big and open to talk

make this day your own square
in your own life quilt
so shining
it brighten the whole of your years this far

make this day like one of God's seven

A Fable

Who say we are our worst enemies?
we are

eye of a thousand faces
we are our loved ones backwards
and the second teller after God who we will be

the stones said to the trees that they should be friends
the trees said they could not bow down that far
the stones turned away to the water
the water said it could not stay still that long
the stones turned to the sky
who said it could not be limited to the color of a storm

the stones then sighed and made silver
cried and set gold
inside their stomachs

and man
he come and worship the stones
more than the trees
more than the water
more than the sky

in fact
he kill these brothers in worship over the stones

how ironic
we make our futures
and always far from what we expect

Kin

Buffalo burned sage
steel jaws around the ankle
high prayers lowered foreheads high noon
these days gone
with my ancestors now long passed

who to carry them
when everyone claim his head too full
who to carry the story
of true things

we walk
empty armloads too full for treasure
thus the old winds must find a new way
into our children's ears

Homecoming

These the Times to Be Strong
for Mohamed

and if you've forgotten
how to stand
return to the Koran
with your brow upon the ground
and remember

On This Day
for Pauline

I

this is a day without chairs
a day where all the rooms melt together
and there are only corners/corners and humming
wishes and slight breeze
brushing you like palms
this is a day of prayers
a day of painful breaking/a day of peace beneath
a day of arms
of hands
eyes and quiet windows

i wish you love from your mother backwards

i wish you deep tunnels without fear
i wish you children's laughter
i wish you cactus flowers
i wish you moonlight
i wish you real eyes
i wish you a hand across your back/soft like when you were a child
i wish you tears
i wish you clean
i wish you angels in conference around your bed holding you
so there is no space for me even to touch you/just watch

i wish your mother watching

i wish you abalone dreams
i wish you peace
i wish you doves in your kitchen
moonlight in your bathroom
candles when your eyes close and dawn when they open
i wish you so many arms across your shoulders

so many lips kissing your ears that you smile from the
    inconvenience
i wish you all your babies' love attacking the center of your heart
just so you know they are there

i wish you banisters, railings, and arms around your waist
i wish you training wheels, i wish you strong shoes
i wish you water o i wish you water
through your feet flowing like a stream
and i wish you hammocks
and melon on your eyes
strawberries in your mouth
and fingers in your hand
fingers in your hand all day
through this house
on this day with no rooms
only corners
and an uncommon breeze

I Will Go

with you
beneath the day to another home
where language so sincere
words cannot contain it
replaced by tides
conversation by rhythms

I will step into the water
submerge all I know how to say
for risk to say it better
in this new place I don't know

where Saturn live next door
air hold my footsteps
my name hold no sound but an exhale of breath
angels cannot fly the air so dense
and color only visit once in a while

to pack my bag is serious
I will do it gladly
at your side I will go
wherever can carry my song to you

Cancer

The end is coming
can see it on every plateau of breath inhaled
Johanna your eldest daughter/a deer
bends for water
at your palm

you Margaret
looking for your peace song
angels writing it
the chorus the first part finished
your son your sister brother mother father they all singing
you the solo
the chorus the first part
the harmony done
the melody they write
pens in hand
Margaret the peace song is in your tongue
dry from open mouth calling in breath
drinking air like kisses
holding time like a big hand

our eyes red
skin pale from being inside
I watch you search for your song
woman on water
looking for the next stone
i witness the growing marks on your cheeks from the rub of oxygen
    tubes
the brows come together like praying hands
the mouth not knowing the right words to say
the direction home or what time
there are hands of a child holding yours

somehow the air tells me not to break this spell not to leave this
    room at 10:15
silver hair mother from apple vinegar rinse
wrinkle wrists from blood stolen by I.V.s those thirsty worms
the feeding tube hangs from the I.V. stand a suitor

your coughs
scraps of sandpaper
we have to wait for you to find your voice

i've had to get used to so many things in its absence
the whir of fans
the grumbling of the oxygen machine
your slow morphine nod growing slower
to tapes of Romans and Corinthians

how fortunate i am to write this while your breath blesses this
    room
I catch it in my hands
like shallow water

Strength

She look like ferns
unwithered after the storm
straight green reaching for God
I want to feel the leaves whisper my cheek and tell me
how it feel to rock
how roots grow with merciless rain

I want to touch her smooth leaves
kiss them wet and feel living

Why Did She Ask Me to Do This?

carry her to the river
make her a blanket to wear over her shoulders
of me and my sister's bones
give her my breath to breathe
roll her hair in rollers and clips
when i don't know how to do it
and she brush my hands away in impatience
and she do it herself in pain and me to watch

why do i have to sweep out that cold room of dead flies and huge
    windows
so that we could wheel her in just for a day

why do i have to give her my horses
white palominos to ride where there is barely any oxygen
so she can make it to God

why do i have to give her my life
lay it down for her to walk on
amongst strangers and two friends

i smile when i see them in her hallways
i wash their dishes i make sure i hang the dish towel just right
i wash all my dishes not only leave them in the drain
but dry them and put them away as if i was not here
i respect their prayer and concoctions of wild beets and aloe vera
    juice
but refused their poison
i played with their children and did her laundry quietly
out of the way

why did you make me lose my peace
take me back to when i was 15

and reading in bed
to hide away from it all

but i made you stories and read to you
rhythms and tones to hold you
when you could no longer hear the words
bury them in your layers
falling into your map
you were making on the way home

i gave you all i could give but a little short
two pieces shy of my whole flesh and bone from you
two pieces shy
i wanted to give up and go home
for a moment i didn't think i could do it anymore
and just then
you left

singing about that great city until your mouth moved
but the words didn't come anymore
and then I knew
you were on the palominos
map and tones and rhythms in your bag and all

and then
blessing the four corners and middle of your room
i knew why you asked us to do this
not only to hold your hand on this side
as you crossed the river
but to give you something new
to tuck in your clothes
to remember us by.

Homecoming

This is a time of sisters
a time of knowing
a time of home
home makes me crazy makes me dizzy
but you call us and we come
in armor of memories
and love

what an honor to help you come and rest
help you find your peace song
Mommy where is your silver throat
where is your company to help take you away
we lay down the little we have for you
to walk on
new sky and grass not green
food I don't know
for this kind no longer works for you at crossroads
and times of goodbye

I am ready
thank you for your iron thank you for your faith
I will look for you in my dreams sometimes
and sometimes I'll leave you alone
say hello to Herbie and Aunt Missy
tell my thank-yous to God
I have no velvet for you
to walk on only me
inside out and ready to give you home

Jesus loves me this I know
for the Bible tells me so
little ones to him belong

they are weak but he is strong
yes Jesus loves me

come angels they come
and your daughters alone

nothing more than children although we always tried to be
we'll leave you now and work on our own paths home
lay it down lay it down
lay it all down

Risk

You cannot discover
new oceans
unless you have courage
to lose sight of the shore

Wedding

A funeral is a wedding with God
betrothed to him
we are at death finally married
his from before the very beginning of beginnings

death a time of white flowers
veils lifted
and love from the whole spirit

i will tell my children
yes wear black on the outside
tribute the scars of this world
but wear light on the inside
for glory of the one who passed

this is the day of celebration
the day of love and arms to wrap you whole
for the rest of your lives

and i will tell you mother that i am proud to help you gather your
    gown
your thread your stitches shoes and stockings
i am proud to be your waiting girl for that day
i apologize if i ever made you feel rushed or uncomfortable
i will remember the preparation and need
i will remember the pre-wedding days
i will remember them past my own
and i will tell my children
i will tell them

Untitled 1

The world ends
to a new place

Momma Died When My Wisdom Teeth Come In

push their way through the holes
not there yet
n stand like a new home

have to
hold my jaw different now

careful when i chew or i cut my cheek
careful how i hold my mouth when i talk
stay away from meat
keep food at the front of my mouth
where i can handle it

dont know how to wield them wisdom teeth yet
just set my jaw in the place it hurt least
and chew

Lungs Don't Lie

I carry my grief
between my shoulder blades
come lay your left palm across
i can take you spinning into tunnels
but you have to get back on your own

this is where i live today
occasional vacations of fresh air
the ocean never looked so sparkled
or air so clean

coming from a room two months filling with cancer

freedom hurt my eyes
fill me with wonder and strange songs
in my head i don't know where they come from

a need to inhale life so strong
i wonder about cigarettes
about making love
but keep my distance from people
a disturbance to my walk
and what follows me like days

i am a newborn
to the same world i left years ago
but it was only seven weeks on the calendar
my lungs cry for something

My Home Looks for Me

bumping into stalls and buildings
she look for my eyes among all these people

this place will find me
same time I find her
we will meet like friends
who never met but recognize each other
hug deeply
and rest

when I wake I will walk with home in my eyes

it could be today when it happens
it could be today

Before I Leave My Doorstep to Mama's Grave

i need to give seven gifts to seven strangers

tuck their good wishes in my new Timberlands
the space between my sock and ankle

i need to walk steady in love
face above the water
an oak tree standing in the middle of the sea

mama i'm not ready to see you yet
in my room
let alone among the headstones
of you
Carrie
and a baby boy i never knew

before i leave my doorstep i need to know peace
so i can bring you some
like earrings
i want to paint the sky in my joy to see you
sherbet colors or
sandpaintings that i used to do on the dining room table

been pushing myself to do each next thing
after you left
go back to school
move to a new house
i can't yet push through another door
my arms hurt from the bruises
my smile strained

let me build my home upon my heart
let me weave my heart into my home

a place to make a nest
when all the straw i know
has turned to grass
beneath my feet a headstone and some roses

let me build my fortress
strong head ready to give seven gifts to seven strangers
open enough to let life in that fickle butterfly
ready to love you like a child
ready to hum you like an old woman
on the porch waiting for God to come down
dressed in all the spirituals she ever knew

let me weave my days in letters to you
write them upon the air in my best school cursive
codes for only you to see
they will say
i miss you, what are you doing, who is combing your hair
i love you
who holds your hand besides your sister
they will say
what are you doing?
i eat cantaloupe on my new balcony
looking down on my neighbor's white pickup
in the morning sun

let me write to you in goosebumps
and a tired neck
let me rock myself steady

i will come like nomads in pilgrimage
i will come in sandbroken feet
i will come in love
and soon
but most importantly in peace.

New Country

Joy seep out like bathwater
down the drain

looking for a place to catch my breath
after Mama lost hers

hid from my tears
covered the heaviness in my throat with laughter
and silence and the guise of ability
lifted new knowledge
pushed myself to new limits that had no room for memories

but my memories
came back to me in dreams
strategizing like guerrilla citizens
planning to take back their country in the night
and now
I am willing to fall like a false government that knew she wouldn't
    last
they take me apart eat me in their palms
and build me back again
every brick every stone every blade of grass
they build me

into a new country
who accept her heart her swollen eyes and sunk throat
emerges like a quilt
strong and conscious
of every hand that made her.

Come between My Knees Child

you with the moon eyes
bring the comb and oil
let me rub it in

Head down

We know this common place this silence
you waiting
for something my fingers to tell you

today they weave a story

we not alone in this place
this is the hour of mothers always the hour of mothers
always with us in this quiet place together
listen
she say be unafraid

Head straight

let your roots lead my fingers
let the mothers dance in that space
no lines tell where you end and we begin

Child you our power

so if the singing break forth
from the oil in my fingers
be unafraid
unannounced uninvited
it is Mama
it is you through the silk in your throat

it is time to leave sorrow together

Pass the ribbons child
you with the moon eyes from crying
pass me all the colors
we go someplace not arrived
in the hour of voices unfolding a new peace

Let It Heal

Listen to the song and let it tell you how
be quiet be quiet be still
let the angels put their hands on where it hurts and
smooth be quiet be still
ask for prayers around you and bathe in song
be quiet be quiet be still
sit in children's laughter twice a day
be quiet be quiet be still
leave your thoughts for another time
wrap yourself in daylight
knit yourself a friend tighter than you imagined
let good people close to you
move away from those that suck from you
be safe be quiet be still

if you have no hands
write
if you have no feet
walk
if you have no voice
sing
and a chorus will carry you
if you have no eyes
see
if you have no arms
hug
be thankful be quiet be still

and the pouring come upon you like holy water
and the healing a new plant

break the ground
emerge clean and willing

sorry and thankful
new and quiet
rejoice
like children at kickball
wise like grandmothers on the stoop
ready to live
and whole
ready
and whole

Venus's Quilt

To the Sea

The moon a dime
in somebody denim pocket
lint with room enough to float like clouds across
how many times does it take to notice/how many days
that dime from half to whole
not enough children to teach us
to look up
at least half our lives
and in the other half

too many ghosts
too many gliding across eyes
too much highway
too many shiny cars

s'all right
i will take me to the beach
lick the waves with my calves
tilt my head back
give the sea my fingers
let it massage my hair
seaweed 'cross my ankles

i will take me to the sea
in my shy bathing suit
looking for someone to hold me and peace
and someone to hold me

Haiku Lost

Give me a kiss slow
So I can forget myself . . .

Someone

is in love with someone
not in love with her
someone sings to the sky
alone
someone walk home
rattlesnakes watching from the path
someone walk barefoot with stones
in her throat

he will love me someday I will grow my hair long
I will slim myself slimmer than an idea
I will walk like breath

and that's what she did
slipped through this world into a ghost
nobody could see
silent woman once in love changed herself
so much
we can no longer find her

Don't Try to Kiss Me into Shape

I've the print of hundreds of lips

in every part of my body

they have bruised me from the hammering
my body tired of angles
I want to learn how to reach upwards
without my hands
I want to dance without a partner
I want to fly without being thrown

Don't offer your lips to me as a gift
your penis a prized possession
don't paint me gold on a rusted nail
I will choose my jewels and they are not between your legs
riding your tongue
or where our hands come together
tired of Band-Aids for my gashes
and promises of cocoa butter

Do not breathe moss into my ear or over my eyelids
I know where I want to step
into the pool of lost stars
alone

gather them one by one onto each bruise and inverted elbow
each broken hip and twisted waist
each bitten lip each slew foot
place them one by one
until I bend my back upwards and disappear
each love bite each moon of a fingernail

that held too tightly
and bring my soul to a place unnamed

I will shed myself
and leave you to play in my skin.

Eagle Woman

She was five she said
when he first molested her
nothing easy like the pages of a book
but rough like sandpaper
he still grate in her ears when she listens

That was years ago
it is water time now
love flows like an eagle between the mountains/she happy
that time no longer a dream every night/more like every five weeks
and if she feel like dropping her shoes and chasing it away
like she did when she was little she can
She can do anything/that's what Mama say
everything but chase away big worn overalls in the night
Where was Mama anyway

Eagles come to her now in years
feathers one year talons the next
soon she will have eyes
to tell her when something dangerous is far away
and coming
a beak to tear it apart if she need to
Eagle woman
she put the symbol on her shoulder/wear it as a scar
no one will touch her again

She will have the eyes
to see it coming/she will have the weapons

To free herself like a wingspan

far above the rocks and petty things who will themselves be eaten
she has no wish to eat rats/mice/rabbits

she will eat only the snakes and the sky
a little sagebrush to keep herself pure and fennel to bring
   the sweet

She will sit in the sunset
at the end of each day
and never remember.

Untitled 2

I had to find my beauty
when it was ready
it came to me

I Could Let You Love Me

Maybe if I let myself
remember those things as part of me
the wild
three-headed strawberries
trees to get caught in
sand hills to jump down
bare legs and scratches
bare feet and teeth
rocks to sit on
and a wide wide windshield

maybe if I let myself
you be my wild strawberries
rich red sugar never a last bite
your arms
trees to get caught in
and never want to come down
each day
the thrill of the jump
simple as ashy knees
we could make a rock steady and always
never a question
is it love sittin there this mornin too
day coming wide with all we could do

maybe if I let myself

Like to Wake Up To

kisses skin eyelashes
good mornins and full body hugs
somebody driftin around the kitchen
gas stove clickin
as water get put on for tea

the sun sweet-talkin her way through my curtains
showin off her new day to play with
as pigeons flutter to rest above my window

Anita Baker Bonnie Raitt Dionne Farris
clean green sheets

rain outside the window
on a day I don't have to get up
just
make myself some cocoa
and go back to bed and read

payday
a day we goin somewhere
children laughin as they try to wake us up
new shampoo new soap
new underwear new jeans new jacket

Friday

a good friend sleeping over
somebody visitin
visitin somebody
peppermint tea with lots of honey
X-men

lips on my neck
brushes of a palm on my hair
eyes looking at me like a friend
discovering something special

you.

Sunday

if i could i would
give you a mirror how i see you
n watch you smile

I Will Show You

I have
no angels in my breasts
only sweet water
but enough to keep you breathing
enough to strengthen your teeth
no rock arms
but enough to hold you when you cry
no plum mouth full of juice and peaches
but enough to give you a garden
and yes i have no orange trees
jus legs enough to wrap you

make me a new world with kalimba songs
hair that will sing back to my palms in chorus and solos
i will show you your grandaddy's storefront
i will show you children playing ball
jacks and grabbing pieces of sunlight
i will reach for conversations between the leaves and the sun
i will show you the seduction of the waves and the moon
i will show you
if you let me
i will show you

Give Me a Kiss

in Diggable pressed G5 please
the last poet who kiss me
lef me spinnin into myself n furious
he promise somethin he could not give

don't ask for promise
just a kiss
the startle of pigeons

in Sankofa bird shadow
rising back to tell the story
of Pharaohs in silk n obedience
of women bowed with straight backs
translating the whisper of candles
age-old always the same
Black people in our own self

this from a kiss
that make my hair wish for naps again
so I could arch for you
make my feet wish for wings again
so I could show you how you send me
make my thighs wish for horns again
so I could call Ntozake
jus to show her I know greens
my bootie wish for drums again
so you could hear me comin
in all my trumpet glory

see i'm lookin for a place to fly into at midnight
n fold into at dawn
a way to sing with my eyes close
and mouth full

a kiss
that fly me off Kilimanjaro
into my ancestors' bones beneath the sea
them callin me
out the top to dance new rings around Saturn
gold this time
from you n me together
spinning the wind we create
from two lips
and God caught in between

Even If I Was Cleopatra Jones

Even if i was Cleopatra Jones
wild cane and sugar in the raw
honeydip dark n lovely gift of the gods
best bootie in the house
and your inspiration

i would not be the one.

i would not be the Nile at the end of your long long day
i would not be your ebony queen in this misplaced land
i would not be the Nubian princess who wanna get wich ya
i would not be the be strong sista
i would not even be poetry brushing past your thigh.
i would not be the stroker of good thoughts above and below
i would not be the guide the wise one the concubine mistress
    partner or best friend
well maybe best friend
but i would not be the one to crawl into or keep safe from myself
hot with the waiting for your mouth chill with the waiting for your
    mouth
naw
i would not be those rose hips on the fly girl round the way straight up
i would not be your world your baby or your mother
i would not be your milk or your honey although i do come close

i would not be any or all or any of these things
if i was yours the one you choose to choose
the one you say you choose
today remember

i would not be any of these things not just at the start of rain
i would not be any of these things. ever.

just the source of some damn good imagination.

No Coast Guard

Your hands blind butterflies
your kiss Indian summer
your body's length a yawn against mine
wake the monsoons
swift me away
no Coast Guard no life station
jus whirlpool
me drowning
with a
smile

Be There for Me

like the sun n the moon
mama n blueberry pie
sunday afternoon
a screened-in porch
one fly
no mosquitoes
n the dishes done

ma legs stretch over yours n
loungin
feel mighty nice
but be there for me
like these socks fallin down like
the lumps in this couch like
the creak in that chair there

be there for me like sisters
like wrinkle fingers after clean
lotion after dry
or if no lotion
Vaseline
smooth
easy
never cold

like Chaka Khan
Chaka Khan who make me feel like livin make me feel like life
when ma throat heavy n lookin for wings

there for me
cuz i am no more a child
mama gone n blueberry pie
not so often

there for me
like this evenin but always
n how i feel so good
blue all mixed up in the air
slow draggin
to you n me n
Coltrane
saxophonin life into itself

n back again
through your lips
full
n sweet
smilin me
into tomorrow

What the Earth Said

I will grow up like a mountain
green and ready
people will wonder where i come from
to become so big

i will be a quilt
patches of earth and root
bushes and rocks
streams
making their way to the bottom

i will crumble sometimes
avalanches falling on those in the way

but in the seasons
i will also sprout
buttercups and dandelions
wild blackberry and raspberry fields
and tall grass for pheasants to get lost in

and i will rain in the nighttime
soft conversations in the sky
and she'll laugh lightning
we will smile about the old times and coming up

i will tell her i come from the country
she will say i am from the city
we will agree it is a little of both
i will whisper in dusk
that i never found love
she will answer with sunset that it was always inside me
and i spent too much time looking
i will agree and go to bed

i will rise with laughter on my lips
she will shut me up with the dawn
we will spend the day wondering
how we all came to be

and so it is until the day we have children
and i will watch
our children the years to come
giving us gifts of creatures
and troubles
anthills and bottle caps
broken glass
guns and blood
they will stain my skin
a million showers will not take the stains away
fires will not burn away the memories
and even sharks will not eat them

we will live long the sky and i
longer than our children
longer than even their dreams
the only thing to live past us
the memories of us all

but even they, they will go
tired of exchanging stories like grandfathers
mending them like mothers
recreating them like sons
they will crawl into themselves and disappear
eating each other until there is nothing left
just God
and his fingers

past that point i do not know what will be
i do not have the vocabulary of future things

nor the mind to make them
all i know is life is forever and ever
longer than fingernails
softer than moss
easier than a baby's smile
more complex than love

life is a lover unto itself
always longing and never ever
satisfied

What the Sky Said

I come lost lightning
stumbling between midnight and morning
you catch me like a light rain

What the Morning Said

My love for you
rising sooner than the east

Venus's Quilt

You need to be loved
I would do it
be the one to open you like pomegranate
take your fruit between my teeth and tongue
and shine every seed
rub you between my palms until the heat come
and the numbness go away
reach into your hair
weed memories that don't belong
and lay out a welcome mat
for all sunshine

there is water in your eyes I want to travel
there is babies to be born yet and shoes to be sewn

if I could I would quilt you into my life
so you could lay just left of my mother
east of my father north of my sister
into my friend

I am Venus without a lover
fingers with soft nails and need to touch
I might ask you to swim in my memory
I might ask you to make your own
we could sit and watch them like slides

how many women should I be
for you to feel loved
how many men
for you to feel safe
how many daughters
for you to feel pride
and sons to be forever

I will be them all
barrettes and butterflies, tube sox and elbows
first drink of water last toothpaste
I will be your uncle's hand
I will be your aunt's kitchen
I will be your sunset in the morning

I am Venus
cluster of grapes in your mouth and wine coming

we are whispers in the length of the dark
we are cuffs in the folds of the universe
I can button you safe
I can hold you forever
so long as you give me your cloth

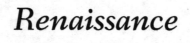

Renaissance

Friend

When we join hands
it is hard to remember
why the world so lonely

When I Saw You Braiding Yourselves
for the seven

I bring old women and babies sucking
half gone butterscotch so smooth
nutmeg skin and scarred knees
give me the oak trees
to scratch my calves upon and leave their mark on me
looking down on the world
somewhere between my brother's fort
and white dinosaurs cruising the sky

Older now
sometimes wonder how my feet continue to plant this earth
why they don't fly from people's eyes
emptying themselves more and more these days
nothing familiar like baked ham brown sugar and pineapple
nothing familiar like black-eye peas and Happy New Year's
with people who tried on the night with you
and stayed years and years in your pocket
nothing familiar like neighbors
children running between your knees
the eyes empty more and more
not knowing how to walk a sidewalk and find a friend
not knowing how to recognize a sister
not knowing who is this brother

so you realize
when i saw you braiding yourselves around this table
i wanted to run my fingers through you
feel myself in the grease we made
shining our spirits to glow onyx and make the night feel shame
so you see
when i saw you braiding yourselves around this table
i wanted to be the knees you sat among

i wanted to be the New Year's
the family you never knew
and you to be them
for me.

Church Y'all

for and with Adrienne, Kim, Lisa, Nyesha, Rhonda, and Sonia

What is it sisters
we was doing there
so long ago
and naming tomorrow at the same time
Strange Fruit playing
and us around a table front of 5th St. Dicks
should'a known better when I counted us seven

what is it we started
playin words but the spirits heard
and decided they would step
into our mouths and out
into the night air
but we were not cold
children
dribbling out our mouth with sweet potato pie
and ice cream brothers six foot nine
black as our table but smoother
corncob pipes sendin messages back to the ancestors
we are still alive

under the ocean rewalking your footsteps
flyin into the sun
on our nipples
brothers stroking the glow on our thighs
speaking
in tongues
funny
didn't feel like seven
felt more like one
but it was us it was we
Black people in the groove

y'all the spirit was
enough for us to get up and dance around that table
like we was a forest for us to sway
with the dip double time like we was children of Moses
on *Soul Train*
and up to the scramblin board
in polyester and black goldfish
chosen to put in our platform shoes
afros seven feet high and black sage
singing after the sunset and before the sunrise

well
Cornel say *So it's true*
Black women can have church anywhere
Holy ghost dance on our hips
as we had to
stop and do the bump
and Kim did the windowpane
Rhonda saw
the double dutch bus comin down the street
we had to stop n
sing it till we couldn't remember no more
n just sit back
sayin
Double dutch y'all Double dutch
Double dutch y'all Double dutch
God turnin the short end of the rope
we found ourselves jumping hand in hand
into the spirit on 43rd Place
43rd Place God picked you to be heaven tonight
Sonia grandmother
Josephine Josephine
came back again
that table home and the kitchen hummin
stories of first times and hmmm
here my ugly stories step out of me

and I thought I was cool with my stories
but here come 17 y'all 17
and my boyfriend's daddy try to get with me
but 19 y'all 19
Nyesha golden verbs dangling
the corners of her mouth
taste a rainbow on Crenshaw

nothin necessary but our tongue and what we remember
seven cleaning women seven housewives
seven orishas curenderas healing women curing women
yes seven healers seven sages
the spirit called itself to us
through the stories singin swayin
like Alvin Ailey's "Wade in the Water"
we was jammin like we saw our mamas at funerals
we was jammin like we did in the hallways at school
Adrienne's eyes close findin the right flow on concrete
we could have sat there for 20 yrs
cymbals rinsing away our days

Strange Fruit droppin up the beats
for us to suck on like butterscotch
y'all made me hungry
y'all made me full
like Lisa say *Black women need to play together*
if we did we would change the world
Black women need to play together like we know how
playin our words like string games like mary mack like freeze tag
like we without age
playing and knowing at the same time
electric sliding into the milky way
to play jacks with the stars
sisters the strength invincible
when we come together in love
y'all gave me love

y'all made me want to shout whole trumpets
y'all made me want to hug everybody down there coming out of
    5th St.

that was church y'all
that was church at 1 am
cuz i got the spirit
smooth enough
for Adrienne to do her James Brown slide
into the jitterbug
on the sidewalk
like it was a dance hall
like it was a school gym
like we was safe
like we was safe in love
we called it to us
life
wanting to talk
twirl its fingers in our hair
feel the sweat of stories traveling to us
after 7 yrs of hiding

Even now the earth shake her head
marking the last days
Death a thief in the night
with more and more keys on his keychain
we losing people under our feet and around this corner
cheekbones crushed into the concrete and left
cuz these are the last days
last breaths of the old world
but us flyin into the new with oxygen masks
from God and the old ones
to let us dance on the cracking sidewalk
chant
our stories together
communal spirit to take us through

we the curtains aflame burning into black holes
we the Nile's children and water
each of us bringing spirit to the table
a cocoon of silver and butterflies already born
with wings of griots.

Peace sisters, peace. i am born again.

Untitled 3

I become comfortable
With my awkwardness
like a swan

You Say My Words Not Mine

to tuck into young beds with kisses and wishes
for dreams sweet as freedom
with unlimited mileage and no down payment
not mine to send down the street
in a new shade of sunrise

you must think I have no nutmeg people
to drink from

Tracie Double Dutch on the Tongue
for Tracie Morris

Tracie Tracie sista girl what you got/what you got
me no words no place n so tired
Tracie Tracie sista girl what you got
n why ma feet gotta itch when you come round
sista girl what you got/double dutch on ya tongue
why my feet gotta itch wich ya rhythm rhythm what
rhythm rhythm what you sayin/we could fly
what you say/you know triple jump off the tongue
what yo name rhythm
well show me wich ya smooth smooth rope/I'll turn

Hand me that rope n us'll turn
one two sista, come on through sista
one two sista, come on through sista

Jump/what you/jump what you/jump what you know
on the concrete/negrita chiquita beat
cuz cornrows don't mean nothin without the grease
gotta have the grease/Dixie Peach/Always
sweet when ya finish
dang
look at ya jagged sunset step/this side of the sea
dookie gold jazz riff waves
lick the street and call feet of heavy hip quick lip sistas
inta vision sharp/rhythm hard n
somehow I know when it gonna kiss the beat
or turn it inside out to teach gravity
how to scat
make me feel like shit ain't nothin this good since Lakeside Stank
i see ya in ya dance
you leadin from the ancestors/cuz they need somethin new
well lead from the ancestors cuz they need something new

call back to the old
cuz rhythm is a place
rhythm is a place you got to step into/to not get lost

I'm steppin in too/to not get lost
one two sista, comin through sista
one two sista, comin through sista

Jump/what we/jump what we/jump what we know
on the concrete
rhythm is a place we step into to not get lost
rhythm is a place we step into to not get lost
rhythm is a place of the ancestors/in our skin n
rhythm is a place of the ancestors/in our hair
high n far out
I said/you got me juiced like a mango/waitin for the right tongue to
sail along/that's what you do just sail along
into the jagged sunset
the sweet/baby/the sweet place/sweet space/I'm in
black feet n ancestors deep in the soles the souls on our tongues
nobody can negotiate/the beat
our feet we free ankles n higher
than rainbows/they swingin
n me turnin/n us turnin/us turnin heads/always turnin
the present inside out
flyin freestyle/lead on sister
lead me on to a fantastic voyage

James Brown/Betty Carter
pack your bags get on up n jam y'all
come on n ride on the funk y'all
hopin for something to pick me up again
me hopin for something to pick me up again
me I was hopin for someone to pick me up again/I was no words n
   so tired
til you come along all sweet n mangoes n no nonsense

in the rainbows/elliptical propellers
freestylin/ma feet /dancin
I/I can/jump in this
double double dutch/double double no single ones
double double dutch tongues
where air is new n sidewalk cracks n feet fly old ways/no single
   ones
feet fly old ways/no single ones
feet fly old ways
in new forms
you teach me the place/the place with no words n alright
me slappin down this/slappin slappin down this
rhythm
present inside out/outside in/to the ancestors
the ancestors/jus holdin me

The ancestors/jus holdin me
one two sista, passin through sista
one two sista, passin through sista

Tracie Tracie what you got/double dutch on ya tongue?
Make me got up again n ready/make me got up again n ready
make me got up again
make me got
up

Malawi Wind Son

for Masauko Chipembere

Masauko
wind's child
nomad looking for his father in his voice
strange harmonies reach diagonally up
bent sideways like rainbows of they own mind
hungry angels reach for this world
ride the river of his guitar

Masauko
wind's child
will you ever find home?

what fertile land do you take me
Malawi Wind Son
harmonies cross each other shaking hands
swimming in the truth

the unity of your voice
make me want to drink it all evening
make me want to stand up and say *Here i am*

Malawi Wind Son
all the searching you do with your song
listening to you
we know we home

Caught in a Hallway of My People
for Ronnie's Ya-Ya Tea Bar

Here y'all go again
fillin me up like the last time
n jus yesterday i said
Somebody catch me
ma dreams are too big to climb

i feel hands in my inside
makin songs
remindin me ma rhythm

here i go
Masa's song *Me and my people buildin* . . .
send me into sways
like sycamore trees
mixed with freestyle
ma hands give fingers where the DJ scratch spirituals
rainbows jump out the side of ma mouth
n where ma feet rest is real again

ma bootie sit on real steps
listen to real words
like oak like peppermints like
honeysuckle on ma tongue
side a ma childhood driveway

Here y'all go
finding ma oceans
here y'all go
holdin me in a cup of hands
Adwin rubbin ma back to Masa's rhythm
snappin fingers in ma ears

reminding me of Renaissance
ain't go nowhere
seep from Nafis's hat
hang in the bite of Adjua's island tenors
roll between the strum of calloused fingers
and fertile throat
nestle in the cave of lungs
caught somewhere between Ronnie's hips and Lisa's nodding head

the dimly lit room full of life n breathing
rhythm and ancestors behind me I can't see but feel
here I am
caught in a hallway of my people
that sway that rhythm
fingerpops handsnaps
click tongues and hollers
fill the night like falling stars
ripple the airwaves
carry me into who I really am
a note in the night's throat
singing a way out of ma fear

y'all give me solar systems inside maself
y'all give ya'll solar systems inside yourselves
ladders and ropes arms and wrists
roots to hold on to

I am in ma natural place to be
full of folks *to the left, to the right . . .*

set it off I suggest y'all set it off I suggest y'all set it off

Here i go filled up again
here i go from your hands
grain for the journey water for the dust

my people whisper me into maself
strong again
i love you

Only God knows how i love you

Healer

You are a healer
like me don't be ashamed
no matter what is in your fingers you will bring it to people
french thyme and apple mint cherry roots blackberry leaves star
    apple words
your lips whatever
Listen to me child get it right what I'm saying
You have whispers the good ones that flow into the heart and stay
    like lace
light enough for someone not to feel you
graceful enough to add peace
intricate enough to add beauty

You are a healer of the highest kind
one who loves her patients
Don't matter what is in your hands how small or soft or wrinkled
You bring peppermint to the scalp and warm hands to the stomach
fawn's ear to the cheeks and breeze
You massage the necks and kiss throats open again
a beautiful occupation and dangerous

Don't take in bitter sweat
Breeze your hands over scars that refuse to go away
keep away from biting sores they will make you bleed
Don't challenge yourself into the fire that will swallow you whole
you are not that strong/maybe one day
For now you build your spirit with the small things

You will be doing this all your life from this world to the next to the
    next
you have time to perfect all your talents
Don't rush your fingers into broken bones don't rush your palms
    into slices

You can walk on fire
but ask for the soles of your ancestors
you can drink volcanoes
but ask for the throats of your mothers who spit fire as well as
    swallow it
you can walk below water
but ask for the lungs of your grandfather Ibo who know the way

All I ask child is never see you alone
We are always with you
If you see you alone you will die
and we will lose one of our necessary children
who we have not taught
so long for this fight
just to be extinguished

The Journey

is a song
black feet protruding the dust covering the water
falling into our souls
the journey is a prayer
find all of us in your song of this world
bringing it closer to where you want it to be
No mind the blood no mind the sweat
babies come and carry on
we do from back when
we do from far forward

The journey did not start from the castles or Middle Passage
it came from us black in the pupil of God's eye
large as the sky and sweet in the humming of the planets
let us carry on
we all pray
the old ones who have been here
the young ones who are not born
we wish to carry your song forward
in all the colors of the earth
if not us who would know blue
who would know the kindness of the sun
who would know green and healing
who would know ice in the waters and fire in the sands
we are the people planted first because we last the longest child
our heart with more depths than Atlantis
we hold the kingdoms lost

pray God we continue singing
pray God we continue the ways of the sticks and the undergrowth
    beneath our feet
pray God we know the waters
pray God pray God

pray God the journey finds us strong as we ever were as we always
   were
pray God the children know which way to go
pray God they recognize each other
pray God the little feet have big ones to step in

The journey long the song to guide us
voices on the left on the right
Solomon's song and Isis's song together in chorus
thoughts and hums arms and angles
chests and necks unshackled
never clear from the path
pray God we see how beautiful we are
pray God we recognize each other
pray God we see ourselves in each other's eyes
pray God you are my harmony
and us walking this world together
teaching it peace teaching it peace
because we have known war

Aché Olumba Alegba Akan
Aché Oshume Lucinte Akan
Aché my little ones my coming my gone
Aché let it be Lord let it be
we recognize each other in our journey
hold each other when we fall
keep company when we run
sing when we stumble
blow when we dust
drink when we rain
pray we bring water to this earth
it is so dry Lord it is so dry
and the little elbows paint the land in your smile
and the little feet dance your song unafraid
and the eyes see each other
and the ears hear your words

and the mouths speak love alone
in a crowded country of your children called this world
we the blood of your breath
the skin of your hope
stones of your fury
tears of your pain
hold your heart in our blues
your joy in our dance

Let the journey continue
let us speak the same language in our many tongues
may the path lead us home may the journey lead us home
in faith child let it be
in faith mother let it be
in faith pop pop
in faith sister
brother my brother let it be let it be
we the sky we the laughter of the rivers
we know day we know dawn we know evening
pray we know ourselves
pray I find myself in you
pray I find me in God
then I know where I'm going and feet to get there

The journey long y'all the journey long
but we got company
pray we find it
know it like our hands
we share
leave it to no one else leave it to no one else
because we took it before time was born
and end it when time is after

Aché little one
Aché

Renaissance
for the World Stage Anansi Writers' Workshop

Who look at this Renaissance
blossoms in our city
like a bruise

beautiful
blues and blacks
spread their hands
past the point of a blow
congeal together in one round voice 360 degrees
in yellows and greens purples and browns
tenors and horns drums and reeds
bass and greasy paper bags
fulla stories brought from home

i say
who look at the chorus
singin up old times and new warnings
who hear the griots staffs scratchin maps and instructions
to constellations warp speed within our nappy heads
who listen to twisted tongues tryin to tell it man tell it
tell it man tell it
the old brothers teach the young ones to break themselves
like warriors in initiation

i say
we weave ourselves into history
with a jacknife
carve a heart into the bark of our people
dig the roots wear them around our necks
clean the dirt from our fingernails
rub it into words for our children to eat

i say
who will name this Renaissance
i stand knee deep in
who go tug the elbow of Langston Hughes
tell him we are yesterday again
to McKay and Cullen and Hurston
Walker and Baldwin
we doin it again
and Sonia
the sisters sing it
to the earlobes
to the temperature of the brothers' heat
watching hips as their hands wander like aimless butterflies
home

who name the round and square faces
who record the clothes
the sandals Florsheims pumps and platforms
singing gelees and just got from the hairdresser curls
twists locks fades and shining heads reflecting the heat of this
    room
padded metal chairs lined up in rows as for a schoolhouse play
who record our applause our sigh our eyes closed and nod
who record a jump up of the spirit an "amen" a "w-e-l-l"
who record our whisper "that's all right" holler and moan
who record our smile our chuckle uncomfortable shift
side glance and elbow jab
stroke beard and rub back
who explain the taste of the room
or how words clearer here
nothing in the atmosphere to hinder them from coming
to our hearts

who will record the music

who explain our convening
to give pictures for our grandchildren

who mark this spot
this door this block that bathroom these chairs
these jazz paintings on these high white walls
this stage 10 inches off the floor
this mike
that knee in the way these hands holding each other
this gray aisle
that green tupperware 3-dollar donation box
his handshake that back slap
her shy smile his hesitation her halting
this stool his stance
this music stand can turn into a pulpit or a bedroom

who name them ours in this home of words
where we walk the halls of each other
and go home like we just seen family

who name these hearts
making scarves for each other
water for the next day
and air and earth to walk on
trading words like baseball cards snappin em like bubble gum
slapping palms and understandings
while
bombs go off daily
and fired workers claim revenge by taking lives
of people they don't know

who will touch
our fine colors reaching into the night air
licking like secret love songs
spreading like a hymn
creeping like a shadow of angry blood
beneath the skin of these times
Los Angeles.

Special Thanks

Lisa Appleberry, Stephen Blake, Anya Booker, Pauline Brooks, Shonda Buchanan, Johanna Forman, Reid-Gomez, June Jordan, Rosalind McGary-Lightner, Celine Parreñas, Lisa Ze, the young magicians, The Anansi Writers' Workshop, Beacon editors Andrew Hrycyna and Margaret Park Bridges, and all those who've helped make this book possible—you know who you are.